C000143981

The Poetry of Peter Banyard SJ

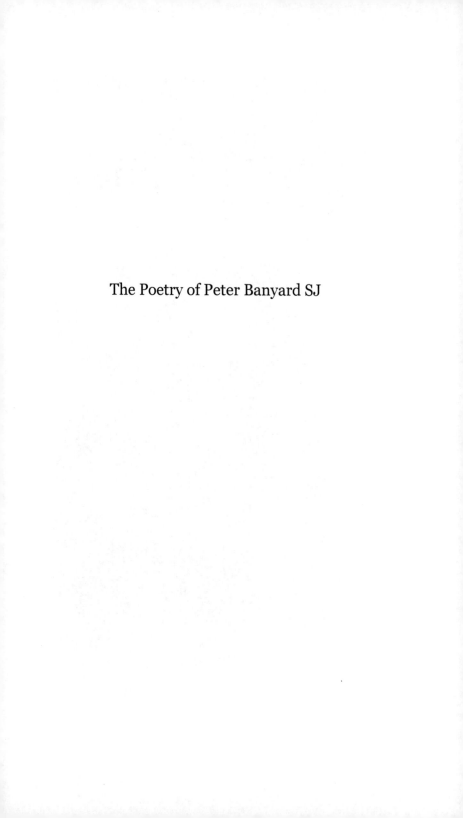

Scholastic at Heythrop College, Oxfordshire.

4, Randolph Rd.,
Glasgow G11 7LG
29/4/21

Dear Tom,

Please find enclosed a copy of Bertie's poem. I'm sorry it's taken me so long to get it mailed out to you.

Anyway here's the book + I hope you enjoy it. Aye, Ronnie

WalterScott250.com

SIR
WALTER
SCOTT
Celebrating
250 Years

The Poetry of Peter Banyard SJ

Published by:

Kennedy & Boyd
An imprint of Zeticula Ltd
Unit 13
196 Rose Street
Edinburgh
EH2 4AT
Scotland
http://www.kennedyandboyd.co.uk

First published in 2021

Text © Clare Banyard 2021

Cover portrait by Simon Davis © 2021
Photographs provided by Clare Banyard, David Ruddy
and Paul Glazier © 2021

ISBN 978-1-84921-215-1 hardback

Acknowledgements

The editor wishes to thank most sincerely the following for their invaluable information, help and advice during the preparation of this collection: Clare Banyard, Felicity Barr, Isobel Boyle, Fr James Crampsey SJ, Dr Frank Dunn, Kenneth Dunn, Paul Glazier, Prof Gerry Graham, Aileen McLaughlin, Fr Dermot Preston SJ, Margaret Renton, David Ruddy.

Football in the pitch at St Aloysius' College.

Contents

x

Fr Peter James Granger Banyard SJ

Fr Peter Banyard SJ, was Chaplain to St Aloysius' College. He died on 7th August 2018 surrounded by members of his own community. He was 87 years old, had been a Catholic priest for 57 years and a Jesuit for seven decades.

Bertie, as he was better known to all his friends, was born in Birmingham in 1931. After a peripatetic school education during the Second World War he joined the Jesuit novitiate at Roehampton in 1948. He undertook the normal formation of the Society of Jesus – in philosophy, theology, teaching and spirituality – and was ordained priest in 1961. He completed his training in St Beuno's College in Wales and in 1963 he was appointed to the staff of St Aloysius' College in Glasgow.

His earliest memory of arriving in Glasgow was hearing Acker Bilk's plaintive clarinet rendering of 'Stranger on the Shore' echoing from a radio in 45 Hill Street. He remarked that that was exactly what he, a distinctive Sasannach, felt himself to be. But this changed very rapidly as he involved himself in the life of what was then an all-boys school and the wider community. When asked his role he would say he taught "religion and rugby football".

Bertie soon became a very effective Games Master organising rugby and cricket throughout the school and inspiring the students with his own enthusiasm for these games. He himself played rugby for the Old Aloysians and was a very popular and well-liked figure among the senior clubs in the west of Scotland and was a much requested after-dinner speaker. He loved the Highlands, even claiming to be related to Flora MacDonald who sailed 'Over the Sea to Skye' with Bonnie Prince Charlie, and so established the Highland Hike for Third year pupils. This was an annual walking holiday to Skye, then Eigg and finally, in 1971, the island of Vatersay which was to become very important to him.

A vital contribution which Bertie made during this first period in Glasgow was to the pastoral care of pupils. Nowadays all schools have elaborate pastoral care programmes involving many teachers, but in the '60s and early '70s it was rare, so in St Aloysius' College a great deal of the provision of this care devolved onto Bertie and he handled it well. He understood young people very well and was very approachable, sensitive to their needs and quick to provide support when required.

In 1976 he left Glasgow to study pastoral theology for a year at Heythrop College in London, before teaching for three years at Wimbledon College and then being missioned as Assistant Chaplain at Manchester University. In 1984 he became a member of the Jesuit retreat team at Loyola Hall near Liverpool.

During those ten years away from Glasgow he retained the Vatersay connection, now without the pupil entourage. He visited the island three times a year, assisting the local parish priest on Barra by taking the Christmas and Easter services, as well as spending three weeks each summer saying daily Mass and ministering to the Vatersay community. His visits became an integral part of island life. The people had great affection for him and placed their trust and confidence in him. For forty seven years he shared their joys and sorrows.

In 1986 he suffered a heart attack at Loyola Hall. When the news reached Garnethill, the then Rector Fr Michael Kyne sent word to ask if he would like to come 'home' to Glasgow. Bertie was delighted with this invitation, and, following discussions with the Provincial, he was missioned back to Scotland and was on the train for Glasgow as soon as he was fit to travel. The following year he underwent major heart surgery – and it gave him a new lease of life.

He was appointed School Chaplain, a ministry he relished. He was the Chaplain to teaching and auxiliary staff as well as pupils and alumni. He celebrated Mass and other liturgical events for the whole school and retained a great interest in the sporting calendar, his aim being always to ensure that the support appropriate to a Catholic Christian school was available to all who needed it. His gentle unthreatening manner, wise counsel, kind words and supportive notes were frequently the tools of his ministry. He thoroughly enjoyed the company of others and he celebrated the marriages of many Old Aloysians, baptised many of their children and grandchildren, and was unobtrusively present to many present and former pupils in times of deepest grief.

He had a special place in his heart for the work of the St. Aloysius' College Children's Fund, a charity which provides holidays for children with special needs: raising money, co-ordinating the students as helpers and giving a welcome rest to caring parents.

Fr Peter Banyard's modesty, wisdom, cheerfulness, his unstinting helpfulness and, above all, his unflinching trust in the guidance of the Risen Lord during his long life have touched thousands. A huge number of these who have benefited from his gifts regard him as a personal friend. That is his miracle.

His Poetry

This book contains a large selection of the poems of Peter Banyard. Most of them were dated by him and have therefore been presented as far as possible in chronological order. The exception to this is the "Hebridean Sequence 1973-1998" which he was keen to keep together as one unit and can be found on pages 9-24

For many years of his later life until 2018 he kept a remarkable series of Lenten Notebooks which were motivated by his desire to keep his writing skills fresh, to reflect on his daily life and to look back into his past. They also give us some insight into the influences which shaped his attitude to poetry and the arts. In his Notebook for 2011 he speaks to his father who had died from a coronary thrombosis when he was only 13, in 1944, to tell him about his life. He tells him how much he had enjoyed living in the countryside and open air in the Worcestershire village of Strensham during the war years, but how all that came to an end with his father's death. Having to move to the town of Felixstowe in Suffolk was for him an unpleasant change.

He goes on to say:

Gone was the life that had centred largely on the countryside. At school I was beginning to widen my interests ... due to one of the De La Salle brothers, Brother Alan. He was extremely keen on cricket and enthusiastic about rugger. He taught Maths but somehow poetry and music came into his classes ... It was reassuring to find that it was possible to be both enamoured of games and of literature and the arts.

(March 20, 2011)

This attitude was further developed when he was a student at Heythrop, the Jesuit seminary in Oxfordshire. In addition to his studies he thoroughly enjoyed rugby and cricket (of which he was team captain) and the return to living in the country:

> At Heythrop it was pure countryside. The spirit of those wartime years at Strensham revived. Time spent in fields and woods made me aware of the fact that I am a countryman at heart. And in this I feel I am very much your son, for I am always conscious that you became more yourself in the country."
>
> *(March 30, 2011)*

The natural world which he describes with such beauty and precision becomes a dominant subject in his poetry from his earliest verses composed during his time as a student at Heythrop. When he moved to the vast industrial city of Glasgow in 1963, he was able to maintain his huge interest in sport as Games Master in St Aloysius' College and at the same time hone his poetic skills on Sunday afternoons when he found inspiration for his writing in the natural beauties of Kelvingrove Park and Pollok Estate. Both of these beautiful green spaces house outstanding art collections in their respective galleries, the Kelvingrove Art Gallery and the Burrell Collection. Their works of art also provided him with subjects for some of his very best poems.

His poems also include portraits of and tributes to many friends and colleagues, including the poet Peter Levi, and descriptions of places dear to him. Particularly striking are "E.N.T. Out-Patients Department, Birmingham 1944", a moving tribute to the nurse who looked after him as a young boy and "To Father Hopkins", a poem praising Gerard Manley Hopkins, the Jesuit Victorian poet whose work he greatly admired and which clearly influenced him. He often gave poems as presents to people on birthdays, wedding anniversaries and other occasions.

And then there was Vatersay. This rugged Hebridean island was undoubtedly his greatest source of inspiration and his poems capture it skilfully in all seasons. Most important of all to him was its people whom he often describes so vividly. At the end of his Lenten Notebook for 2011 this is how he describes it to his father:

That island has been an integral part of my life for over the last forty years. It is a relatively small island with some hills and some wonderful beaches. Above the beauty of the place is the population. I have been welcomed by these Gaelic-speaking people as if I was one of them. You would enjoy their company: realists in a climate of gales and rain, humorous, proud of their families and their history, they are a most attractive people. I should have introduced you to them much earlier, for Vatersay, people and island, has influenced my life considerably over the past four decades."

(May 2, 2011)

As a Jesuit Peter Banyard the poet saw the world through the lens of St Ignatius, the founder of the Jesuits. Like Gerard Manley Hopkins he saw God in everything and good in everyone. To the end his poems bear testimony to his great faith as can be seen in this quotation from the last poem in this collection. As well as being a birthday present to Claire Campbell it is dedicated to the memory of his old friend Donald Duncan Campbell and Eilidh MacLeod, a victim of the atrocity at the Ariana Grande concert in Manchester in 2017:

> Vatersay's soil, sandy and soft,
> affords the dead a peaceful resting place
> until the Resurrection trumpet sounds.
> Then will the aged arise rejuvenated,
> the young their vitality and grace resume.
>
> That our sadness may be changed to hope
> we turn to the risen Christ and Our Lady of the Waves.

Ronnie Renton

The Poetry of Peter Banyard SJ

Before concelebrating outdoor Mass on Vatersay.

Rooks

Rooks
That homewards go
Towards tall trees
In stillest even;
Crossing the dimming sky
In loud procession.

Rooks
That have flown
O'er English fields
For centuries
As the sun dies slowly
Beyond the woods.

Rooks
That alone are worthy
To rest in high elms and oaks
Which stand for ever
Sentinels of our sacred shires.

1952

September Afternoon, Heythrop

Beyond the dreaming trees in rows
It stands, stone Cotswold grey,
A sleeping village church
Where ancient spirits pray.

Heedless of the passing years
They have not felt the world
Grow old with death, decay,
They with angels' wings unfurled.

They remember only Spring,
And the surge of youth in bud
Before the trees grew old
And harsh winds chilled their blood.

Softly now the sun may shine
While rooks wheel and cry;
Church and trees, unlike these
English ghosts, will dream and die.

1959

Crucifixion: Heythrop Cemetery

Christ hanging from a tree:
No muttering soldiers and clicking dice for company;
Only the silence left by departed rooks
And the quick descent of September dusk.
No crimson comfort of a coloured day;
Only the sullen grey of the clouded West
And the soundless flutter of the falling leaf:
No broken woman with a sword-pierced heart:
Only the hooting of a distant owl
And Christ dead upon a rotting tree.

c. 1960

Heythrop: On The Green Bridge

Stillness:
No coot or fish
Ripples the pitch-black pool
That lies like a shroud over the sunken sunlight
Lost in a deep beyond all seeing.
Only a leaf floats for remembrance.

c. 1961

Heythrop: September Evening

The pale sun set an hour ago,
Now late rooks make haste
Across the fading afterglow.

I have no eyes to see outspread
These banners of the passing day,
Yellow, orange touched with red;

But darkness, rising in the hollows beyond
The stream, to greet the lonely stars
Soon to bejewel the silent pond.

This darkness does the woods enfold
Where proud, reluctant oaks must shed
The last sere leaves of autumn gold.

c. 1961

On the West Beach, Vatersay.

Vatersay: A Hebridean Sequence
1973 - 1998

Vatersay Bay

I see in a shell
A stretch of shore
Where tiny translucent waves
Softly smooth the sand
As if each grain were gold.

I see in a shell
The sky paling yellow
Towards twilight;
Darkness a hint, not a threat,
On the assurance of a solitary star.

I see in a shell
A world of wildness
Distilled to delicacy
Watched by none
But a lonely floating gull.

April

Two Poems

Jonathan

Planting potatoes one April Day,
Wizened hands gently on the spade,
You spoke of the wide world you'd seen
And pointed to the place where you'd be laid:
The fenced-off field studded with stones
And crosses midst flower-filled grass,
Said you would nowhere else wish to be
Waiting on time into eternity to pass.

Neil

Your gnarled hands put coals carefully on the fire
Making a chore a religious rite.
Then you sit and light your pipe.
'Peggy probably won't be here
When you come again.'
Words gently spoken,
Marking the sunset of a life-time's love.
Outside the window
The light is fading in the West
And tears well slowly in my eyes.

Summer Fragments

WEST BEACH

Low tide leaves a skein of sky
Stretched across the sands
Between the dwindling breakers
And the indentations of the dunes.

Beyond broods shadowy Sandray
And the ever present past.

AUGUST NOON

Shadows of seagulls
Float across the face of cliffs
Whose feet long waves caress
With blue and green and purifying white,
Assuaging in this summer noontide
The wanton wounds of winter storms.

AUGUST

This rare summer day
I dream on warm rocks
looking westward
where a few clouds, hand-sized and harmless,
hang motionless above a sunlit sea.

Beyond the sharp rimmed horizon
sail the ships that simply pictured
hang now proudly framed on kitchen walls.
Sturdily they steam through brightly coloured waves,
funnels streaming thick black smoke
over the stiff ensign straining at the stern.

These merchantmen were crewed by my Island friends
Roderick, Jonathan, Calum, Donald John and Neil,
centuries of sea-going in their blood,
who softened all the corners of the world
with their gentle Gaelic voices;
who enriched me with their wisdom
in the evening of their lives.

A small breeze touches my face,
dissolving the dream.
The ships are long since sunk or scrapped
and my friends are berthed a mile away
under a pall of rough grass and wild flowers.

Hebridean Burial

In memoriam D Mac N

The rain relents.
Clouds run raggedly just above the low hill.
The brief midwinter afternoon shrinks into evening.

The mourners gather with the dusk around the coffin;
Dark, timeless figures kneel anonymously
In the wet grass.
The final prayers hang but momentarily in the wind.

Suddenly a blackbird, a field away,
Interjects a few notes of resurrection.

Strong arms are swiftly filling the grave,
Each spadeful of sandy soil falling
Certainly, silently like tears.

As we walk away
Waves on the mid-distant shore
Pound out their own relentless recessional.

Graveyard

Borve, Isle of Barra

I walk among the dead
buried on this windswept point
unperturbed by the pounding of the waves
which crash and spume on rocks
beyond a drystone wall.

Here amongst the island dead
lie sailors of two wars
freed from crumpled steel,
with only wheeling gulls
and the shrill lapwings' call.

Around these peaceful dead
the sheep graze forgetful
of their new-born lambs,
symbols of the Resurrection
of him who died for all.

Dusk

Only the harsh call of the heron
Echoes through the loneliness
Of the Hebridean dusk:
Grey waters bear motionless
The leaden images of half-hidden hills
Merging with the mist:
Night comes, dissolving distances into darkness.

Vatersay 1994

Visitors process along the road in cars
Beneath a hill whose glacial scars
Are smoothed by the wind and the rain.

But I know where at the foot of the hill,
Nestling beside a heather-shielded rill,
Each Spring the first primroses flower again.

Primroses

Not here the coiffured head,
The tailored stalk
Set among the ordered leaves
In well-groomed borders:
Soft petals, pale as watery sun,
Shrink from the spindrift wind
Which combs the cliffside grass,
And signal beauty in their brief fragility.

Seashore

The sea surges and sucks,
Creaming in crevices
Of riven rocks.
White water, washing
Reed-green walls,
Wells, then drops.

Ceaseless sound rising
And sinking
Lulls with variable violence
My restless mind to peace.

Vatersay Relics

Where the broken fence
Crosses the rutted path
Lies a cylinder block
Beside a sheep's skeleton:
Both bleached to whiteness,
Mineral and animal,
By the unselective elements.

January 1995

Gannets

Huddled on dark rocks
I gaze across an empty Atlantic.
Clouds promise imminent rain.
Three oyster-catchers stand sentry some yards off.
Beyond gannets circle, then drop.

Lying on firm sand
I look across the Sound to Sandray.
A hesitant sun makes brief appearances.
Twelve terns in single file preen themselves at the tide's edge.
Beyond gannets weave, then dive.

Perched on the far Point
I rejoice at the sight of the sparkling Minch.
The wind is Autumn in August.
An occasional gull passes casually by.
Beyond gannets soar, then plunge.

Winter Fragments

I remember
Five swans rising from the winter lochan
And my senses numb in the frozen air:
The deliberate spread of tapering wings;
Long, thin necks straining to the North.

I remember
Five geese standing near the low Point
And quietly conferring amongst themselves:
Then, the cackle cut,
They head for the estuaries in the South.

....

On this shortest day
Brown land and dark rock lie soaked
Sandwiched between grey skies and grey seas,
Whilst the sun describes its lowest arc unseen.

....

Never sunset in the sea
But always the cloud
Stretched across the horizon,
Tinged with orange, yellow, red,
As black seabirds,
Precursors of the night,
Skim the waves to the west.

March 1992

Poem For A 90th Birthday

For C Mac L

'That's the way of the world' you said
And the world seemed a world away
As you sat looking out of the window
On that cold but sunlit day.
Over the loch and the hill plovers wheel
Calling to lamb and to calf as they pass:
The wheatears flit and the skylarks sing
And little low primroses hug the grass.

Vatersay, Easter 1998

Return To Glasgow

'The passage smooth, Oban dry, the train punctual.'
Thus to one I wrote, saying
Nothing of the waste of waves
Into which the Islands slowly sank
In the low, cold December sunlight:
Nothing of the ghosts of summer visitors
Untouched by the eddying winds, the falling dusk,
The empty bay, the deserted promenade:
Nothing of the hours of tunnelled darkness,
Rattling blindly past hills and lochs
To arrive at a station which was terminal.

Invigilation: French 2A

In ordered rows you sit
Frowning at French.
Outside the Monday morning rain
Greys out the memory of Sunday.

I think of waves,
Blue in the March sunlight,
Breaking on ragged rocks
Into creaming foam of ultimate whiteness:
Waves surging and searching the clefts and crevices:
Perpetual movement and music.

Your pens write relentlessly:
Outside in the street
A car splashes up the cobbles:
Dogs bark.

I see the waves
Kiss and caress the sands,
And beyond the bay the sea stretches
Into infinity: time is irrelevant:
The centuries are encompassed by the mind,
And beauty grips the heart.

Glasgow 1975

English Examination

Invigilation is introspection ... ...
Marvelling how my mind
Engenders ideas idyllic
Which into the thread of unspoken words unwind
And loose the memory's senses
In such ways that it is only I who knows
The incommunicable beauty felt –
Oh! the sight, the scent, the softness of a rose.

Wimbledon, May 1978

In Medio Non Stat Virtus

Your young men shall see visions,
Your old men shall dream dreams   Joel

In suspended time
Between visions and dreams
I take stock on the raised plateau.

Below, the patchwork woods and fields
Fade in the floating shadows of the clouds.
I look fearfully towards landmarks
Never to be revisited,
Strain in vain for the lark song left beneath.
Ahead, unattainable but beckoning yet
The high peaks stand,
Divine predicates of prehistory and eternity
In my piecemeal world.
The wind rushes in dark waves
Through coarse grasses beside dried up pools.

How far shall I go before the darkness falls,
On what gentle slopes begin my dreams?

At The Top Of The Roman Steps (N.Wales)

Peering precipitously at a pool,
Bland and black, cupped in a coomb,
I muse on the mystery of the millenia
Spent in the moulding of mountains.

Brushing the surface briefly, a breeze
Ruffles into ripples the ever-inscrutable water:
Cloud-shadows as they slide across hills
Speak naught but of the softness of this September noon.

Manchester, November 1980

Barmouth Revisited

The shoreline lures the reluctant gaze
Towards the middle distanced peninsula
Taking the eye from the seaward horizon,
As the immediacy of today curtails the vision
Of an unseen future.

It was not thus those thirty years ago
When the meeting of sea and sky
Challenged the imagination with hope unbounded,
Drew the mind beyond Atlantis to undiscovered Americas.

Now I shrink from images of infinity,
Take refuge in the waves' affirmation of eternity.

Manchester, March 1981

Depression

I have naught to offer but my nothingness
No thought burgeons in the frosted air,
The mind as dark as a starless night
When the wind from nowhere
Provokes the brittle protest of leafless trees.
The heart is empty as the estuary,
Mat mud under a leaden sky,
The tide shrunk out of earshot,
And the echo of the last lone bird
Long since erased from the memory.

Manchester 1981

Autumnal Alliteration

Beside the beech hedge
The herbaceous plants hang
Deflowered and dying,
All energy expended.

A late, lone lupin
Of palest pink
Is a token taper
For the summer's obsequies.

Kelvingrove: Early February

Whilst Kelvin ponders with pen poised
Seeking the precise word
Which could measure
The flow of polluted river waters,
Lister lifts his eyes to the low sun
Laying softly on the stark trees
And the rimed grass a down payment
Of pale gold for the Spring to come.

Glasgow, 1987

Art Gallery, Kelvingrove

The sky lies on the roofs
As rain slate-grey and straight
Rebounds inches from the street.

I escape up the stairs
To where Monet's countryside
Shimmers in the summer heat.

Glasgow 1987

The Shepherd

Wearily I'd watched the sun sink beneath the bars
Of coloured clouds; the silent stars
Came to speckle the airy blackness of the midnight cold
Whilst my sheep, uneasy, shifted in the fold,
Till suddenly by angelic song beguiled
I found myself kneeling before a new-born child.

Glasgow 1987

Remembrance Sunday, Glasgow

I walk unsheltered from the drizzling rain
Through the bare November park.
Black skeletal branches stretch
Above the sodden mass of unswept leaves.
Beyond the muddied Kelvin,
Flowing faster than the Aisne or Somme,
The faint strains of a piped lament
Come to fester the memory.
Once more I am haunted by my father's fears,
His battle dreams,
Filtered to me through the lines of Owen and Sassoon.

A small, hand-made poppy, bright-blood red
Focuses the mind's eye on all those dead.

Glasgow, November 1989

Second Spring

Stagnant water in a disused canal
Black with a century's sunken images
Fails to reflect the conversion of warehouses.
The blaster's sand erases industrial grime:
Black, barred, sightless windows are filled
With small, bland panes of glass,
Whilst within tradesmen fabricate
New Victorian luxuries.
Where once barges berthed waterbirds ply to and fro;
Moorhens thrust with self-important strokes,
Coots nod unabashed by baldness,
Mallard drakes flash reminders of another world;
A swan sits again on last year's nest.
Along the banks,
Amidst the flotsam of a tin and plastic age,
Young reeds are upwardly mobile.

Glasgow 1990

Garnethill

A full moon,
High and prismatically haloed,
Sheds a softening light
On sandstone tenement houses.
An old woman
Shuffles along the pavement
Urgently calling her cat
Which materialises, a pale Orlando,
From beneath a 'permit holders only' car.

The wind, changeable and chill,
Ensures an otherwise empty street.

Glasgow 1992

At The Burrell

Steep sunlight from above
Falls on the Virgin's crown,
Lighting half her face.
The sharp shadow of her Child's hand
Rests weightless on her breast.

Glasgow, 1993

A Corner Of The Burrell

INSIDE
The past is held in ivory, wood and stone:
Mary, the Christ-Child, a selection of saints.
Time arrested by the artists' tools.

OUTSIDE
The present pulses in grass, flower and tree:
Bluebell, bud and unfurling leaf.
Time untrammelled by the hand of man.

Glasgow, 1993

Afternoon Tea, Glasgow

Four o'clock dusk
And my step slackens
Passing a terrace of late Victorian houses.

Uncurtained windows reveal high ceilings,
Corniced and ornate,
Some stark in fluorescent light.
Girls at desks peer at little screens.
Is each machine, I wonder, processing the past?
Are they watching, this selfsame hour,
Heavily shaded lamps letting the coal fire
Cast dancing shadows on the walls?
Do they see silver teapots on a silver tray:
Delicate tea services:
A dish of buttered scones kept warm by the grate?
Do they hear the hostess ask
"Milk or lemon in your tea?
Sugar? .... One lump or two?"
A gentle pull upon the bell and
"Some more hot water, Morag, please
                    ...... As I was saying ......

                                        · *Glasgow 1993*

The White Cart Water

A low sun drained of summer colour
Filters a pale light through leafless trees
And is reflected in a river-mirror
Rippled not by wind but ducks.

Glasgow, December, 1993

Ward 9B, Stobhill

"We're not monitoring his heart"
I hear the staff nurse say
As I lying bored upon my bed
Gaze at my feet all day
Wondering what links my arrhythmic beat
To those pedestal and lever feet.
Can the monitor read my heart
And the names so much of it a part?

Glasgow, 1994

Ross Hall

For J C P

The house stands sightless,
A sandstone monument to Victorian wealth
Wrung from the teeming banks of Clyde.
What once was garden is now public park:
Mown lawn, bordered by shrubs and evergreens,
Runs down to brown, muddy ponds
Where two mallards swim sad, dutiful attendance.
Spring birdsong carries the echoes of Eden
Till the lifted gaze sees beyond
Where, drab and lifeless, council flats
By their silence proclaim the post-industrial age.

Glasgow, April-June 1994

St Beuno's, 1994

A summer's week in Wales
Fragments in November's memory.
There was honeysuckle in hedgerows
Scenting the July air.
In a wood all was motionless
Save for one nettle leaf trembling.
A smiling girl rode a white horse
Down a tree-tunnelled lane.
A frenzied little owl harangued
A herd of cows from a half-dead tree.
A squirrel lay sprawled sunning itself
On the arm of the cemetery cross.
By the roadside, midst meadowsweet
And purple vetch, wild strawberries grew.

Glasgow, November 1994

Kelvingrove, 1994

Late November
And the sun gone by half-past three:
Only the elms, future victims to disease,
Have yet to doff their autumn livery.

On the river a random convoy of leaves
No longer floats downstream.
Blackbirds scold from bush to bush,
Whilst beyond the Park lamps begin to gleam.

Glasgow, November 1994

Cemetery, Winchester

Tucked away in the far corner,
Beside the low wall,
Beneath the straggling bush
Where the robin elegizes in Autumn,
My mother lies.

Glasgow 1994

December Night, Caolas (Vatersay)

I stand at the side of the winter lochan.
The wind, ruffling the sheet of moonlight,
Carries the quacking of unsuspected, unseen ducks.
Around me loom dark shapes of grazing cattle
And from the westward comes
The incessant sound of the sea.

Poem For Mary and Catherine

Elegant in black
And the full flower of womanhood
You were setting off for the Charity dance.
I cast an admiring eye.

I recalled that day,
Two decades and more ago,
I came across you sitting in the dunes.
We talked.
I wonder now what we said,
There in the sunlight and slow tempo
Of a summer's afternoon.
Was the future then an unspoken teenage dream?

The sun, the sand, the marram grass;
The soft sound of breeze and sea:
The memory is still vivid, fresh,
And gently touches the heart of me.

Cafeteria, The Burrell Collection

Ageing is needing my four o'clock tea
And sipping it slowly beside the window
As I watch the December world
Deprived of detail by the gathering dusk.
The onset of winter no longer saddens
Now that sixty have come and gone.
Hope has become habitual,
Certain as the coming of another Spring.

Glasgow, 1995-1996

Statue

The Virgin – limestone, fourteenth century, Ile de France —
Stands regally erect, calm, serene,
Her child upon her arm.
She smiles:
He gazes through the plate-glass wall,
Enchanted by shafts of sunlight dappling the grass
Beneath the towering trees beyond.
In his hand he clasps - is it tiny orb or apple?
I think the latter: a reminder of a race to be redeemed,
A Kingdom of grace to be restored.

Glasgow, 1995

1st July, 1996

Zero hour is the sun scrambling
Over the mountain top,
Glazing the damp green grass,
Glistening on a scattering of rocks.
A westerly wind, brisk and fresh,
Ruffles the sea-loch surface.

On this Highland summer morn
My mind is haunted by history
And the slaughter that was the Somme.
Eighty years on the sheep safely graze
But the yellow irises are yet
Flickering candles for the dead.

Glasgow, January, 1997

The End Of Days: Three Fragments

ENGLAND - 1961

Day, paling into pastels, dies with dignity in the West
As silence and mist creep up from the stream:
Dusk unveils one by one a canopy of stars
And reality assumes the delicacy of a dream.

WALES - 1984

Bruise-black, blood-red, lemon-yellow
The day yields in an agony of colour
Pressed upon the hard horizon of the hills.
Yet on the morrow?
White light and resurrection in the dawn.

OUTER HEBRIDES – 1997

Never sunset in the sea
But always the cloud
Stretched across the horizon,
Tinged with orange, yellow, red,
As black seabirds,
Precursors of the night,
Skim the waves far out in the West.

Vatersay: Two Ends And A Beginning

31st December, 1997

    The year has but six hours to run
      As the wind clears the sky
      To reveal the new born moon
      Now sinking beyond the western hill.

31st December 1998

    Hunched in a niche in the dunes
      Above the deserted beach,
      Scanning the empty bay
      I watch the short day fade
      Whilst waves, clean-topped, grey-green,
      Roll inexorably in to crash
      And thunder into seething foam.
      A year ends and all the gulls have gone.

1st January 1997

      The New Year is three hours old,
      The air breathtakingly cold;
      The line between sea and land
      Tiny waves lap-lapping on the sand.
      The last-quarter moon at my back
      Casts a shadow sharp and black,
      As into the future I stride purposeful and fast
      Yet ever haunted by the Hebridean past.

Glasgow, February, 1999

In Memoriam, Mary MacLean

Forgive me my fears:
That the "cheerio, just now"
Was indeed a last farewell.
You sat so calm beside your bed,
Making that corner of the ward
A place of warmth and peace.
You thanked me for coming
Just as you always did
When I visited you at home.

At home: you sitting – "happy as a queen"
You always said – upright in your chair
And a rosary lying in your lap.
Then I, leaving outside the wind and rain,
Would sit beside you in the firelight.

Sometimes you spoke of long ago:
You and the Barra girls gutting herring
Round the East Coast ports:
Hard work, companionship and laughter.
Then the years of domestic service
In hotels or douce Glasgow homes,
Before the return to Vatersay, marriage,
A family and an ever open heart and door.

At The Burrell Collection

Beside a pillar stands
A pale French limestone Madonna:
Tall and crowned
She proudly holds her lively child:
Her love is in her smile.

Beyond, against the wall,
A German painted limewood Pietà:
Racked and bowed
Mary cradles the corpse that is still her Son:
Her love is in her tears.

23rd June, 1999

Stained Glass Window

For John and Hania

A tall Christ
Hangs crucified
In plain translucent glass

The sharp April sunlight
Touches the few sober colours:
The yellow thorns which enwreathe the head,
The cobalt cloth around the loins.

Five centuries ago,
In a softer English Spring,
Simple folk in some pillar-shadowed nave
Gazed upon their Lord
Framed in a chancel window.

Ivory Statuette

A crowned Madonna
Sits, scarce two inches high,
And a little child
Stands laughing on her thigh.

Carbeth

A hawk hanging in the moist air,
The heron statuesque beside the loch
On which float motionless a pair of swans,
Match the palpable silence of coniferous woods.

Glasgow 1999

Pollok Woods

MAY

Chestnuts hold candles for your Son,
Bluebells make a carpet for your feet,
Blackbird and thrush your beauty laud,
In your arms God and mankind meet.

MID-DECEMBER

Slender trunks of tall trees
Silhouetted against pale blue skies
Are still witnesses to nature
Pared to essential form.

Yellow-wash sunlight
Softens the starkness,
Presages the coming solstice
And the Word made flesh.

Glasgow, February 2000

Website

Any early autumn morning,
The air crisp and clear:
The sun's first level rays
Touch the hedgerow hung
With spun gossamers
Bejewelled with dew.

March 2000

Speir's Wharf

Clouds stone-grey and
Cobbles matching the clouds.
Ice a grey cover over black water
Where no wildfowl swim.

Two swans preening,
Grey gulls standing:
Only my own breath moving
In the windless air.

Glasgow, 17th January 2001

Prinknash, 10th February 2000

Kyrie eleison,
Christe eleison ...
The ancient chant still echoed in my head
As I walked down the path to the tree:
An ash many decades old,
Tall and splendid in the chill air.
Around the trunk snowdrops flowered,
Pure in their transient beauty.
The rain had cleared and beyond,
Westward, lay the sunlit plain.
February is the month of mortality
And the first faint hope of another Spring.
                    Requiescas, Petre, in pace.

30th January 2001
For the poet's friend Peter Levi, poet and scholar

Larach*

Down from the Dun
The old house stands
Amidst a tangle of wild flowers and weeds,
Rugged walled but roofless,
A tumbling testament of eviction.

This summer afternoon all is quiet:
The larks have descended into silence,
The corncrakes rasped until they can rasp no more.
On a gable end
A thrush settles
And gently pours forth
A stream of notes
That in their delicate clarity
Unlock a timeless beauty
That draws the mind to God.

*Larach (Gaelic) ruin

Vatersay, July 2001

October Afternoon

St Swithun's, Martyr Worthy

I sit in the silence and peace
Distilled by centuries of prayer
Within these Norman walls,
Listening for the hushed voice of God.
All I hear through the open door
Is the conversational cawing of rooks
As they forage in the fields
Beyond the river and the wood.

November 2001

January

For D L

I walk home in the deepening dusk
Past indefinite shapes of trees.
A thrush thrills the upper air
With impromptu beauty
Whilst in a bush a blackbird scolds.
I look forward to lengthening days.

Glasgow 2002
For Deidre Levi, widow of Peter Levi

For Francisca: An Engagement Offering

The pale wash of midwinter sunlight
Softens the starkness of skeletal trees.
I walk to the woods in their silence
Leaving behind the water running over the weir
And the chattering jackdaws afield.
I stand in this moment of peace,
Poised between Autumn and Spring,
Knowing that love has no seasons.

Glasgow, 13th January 2002

May Day, Kelvingrove 2002

Thump, thump, thump,
A monotonous beat,
Thump, thump, thump
Hammers the head in the evening air,
Thump, thump, thump,
The deafening end to a May day march.
Nearby steel band discs, lorry borne,
Lend an incongruous Caribbean note.
At the far corner of the Park
A piper plays,
Conjuring up a whole history of
Scotland and the clans.
Meanwhile with sweetness unalloyed
The blackbirds blithely sing.

Glasgow, May 2002

Quarr 22nd July 2002

(The abbey was dissolved 22nd July 1536.)

Cistercian ruins cast long shadows
Aslant the undulating field
Beneath whose sheep-cropped grass
Lie the bones of long-buried monks.

Was the sunset slow beyond the Solent
That day of Dissolution?
Were the rooks, in ragged ranks,
Streaming loudly homewards?

Still the sound of "Salve Regina"
Hangs hauntingly in the evening air.

August 2002

For 1st February

(Peter Levi's Anniversary)

The tracery of winter trees
Against a deepening sky
Which has an expectancy of stars;
The whistle of unseen ducks in flight
Awake yet sunlit memories of the past.

Glasgow, 31st January 2003

Kelvingrove, 2003

A heron stands on a half-sunken branch,
Erect, regal, would-be ruler of the pond,
Making grey into a distinctive hue.
Just beyond him floats a swan,
All purity and grace,
Dipping a disdainful beak
Into uninviting waters.
Round about the multi-coloured mallard
Swim with a purpose known only to themselves.

Glasgow, April 2003

Implementation Strategy

Let the earth bring forth vegetation ... let it bring forth living creatures.

What strategies to implement? What schemes of work?
What do you assess and how?

Expressionless the school staff sit
Seemingly unmoved by 'criteria for success'.
The amateur goes to a professional grave.

Depressed I homeward go through the Park
Where grass looks more green than ever before:
Sunlight silvers the peat-brown river:
The wind tosses the chestnut candles,
White candles pin-pricked with crimson,
Pink candles delicately daubed with pale gold.
All the while blackbird and thrush
Sing unscripted, careless songs.

My heart quickens at this implementation
Of the paradisal strategy that God began.

Glasgow, May 2003

Untitled

For R and M

My desk gives refuge to unread books,
unanswered letters, a clutter
of pens, ink bottles, Vatersay pebbles,
a little Arran duck, a broken watch,
a paper-weight, a yet-to-be-eaten apple
and flourishing in an ornamental glass
golden buttercups with tall stalks of grass.

June 2003

Full Moon: 31st July 2004

The red moon just risen
casts a bronze beam
of narrow light
across the windless bay.

Climbing to clarity
her light shatters
into a glittering path
of little dancing silver waves.

All the while the tide
laps tenderly on the rocks
and the black shape of Meall
stands solid against the sky.

Vatersay, August 2004

In Memoriam: Ruaraidh MacClennan

Our first meeting I remember well:
You sitting that summer's day at your daughter's door,
I coming down from the Dun
Wading knee-deep through wild flowers and weeds.
All the while lark song filled the sunlit air.
You sat there smiling, at peace
After your life's long adventurous voyage,
Safe now in the harbour of old age.

Vatersay, 2005

E.N.T. Out-Patients Department, Birmingham 1944

Did I bring you flowers?
I, who with my but thirteen years
Was reticent and shy,
Came in from a countryside
Luxuriant with wild, May flowers.
I came for the dressing of my wound.
You each time with gentle dexterity
And gentle, reassuring words
Probed and cleaned and dressed anew.
I was perhaps a little in love with you,
You with your black, black hair
And dark, dark eyes, your voice
With the music of some green Welsh valley.
After sixty years I forget your name
But still I hope I brought you flowers.

Glasgow, June 2005

For Peter's Anniversary

Reading old letters
I open a door on the past
And hear your laughter and your voice.
Those were the days of exploration:
of a world of deepening friendship,
of poetry and of learning lightly worn.
Always there were larks ascending in the sunlit air.

Glasgow, January 2006

By Pollok House

The bitter week-long wind has died:
Mild air brings faint hints of spring.
Small birds punctuate nest building with song.
From some yet skeletal tree
A thrush pours music
Over the first diffident daffodils
That nod beneath the avenue of limes.

Glasgow, March 2006

Visitation

Mary hastened on her way,
Veil blowing in the late March wind,
An overnight bundle in her hands.

Now in medieval wood or stone
wearing either coronet or crown
with the Christ child regally she stands.

Glasgow, May 2006

Late Summer

For M and L

The peat-brown river,
belying its title of White Cart Water,
mirrors perfectly
a September sky,
pale blue with a hint of haze:
and trees awaiting the yellow
touch of Autumn's brush.
A lone leaf floats at barely perceptible pace –
all the while the present
becomes irrevocably the past.

Glasgow, September 2006

In Learning Support

For S B

Looking North
I sit and dream
Watching the sunlight slip along the hills
Following ever-elusive shadows.
The past comes trickling into my head
And oh! so slowly floods the mind
With gentle memories of friends of long ago.

Glasgow, March 2007

Water Mill, Pollok House

For R and M

Slow-moving, peat-brown the river flows
Between bush-bounded banks,
Bearing the shadows of attendant trees
That lie gently on the sunlit surface.
Suddenly the weir-white water tumbles
Into foam-covered swirlings and eddyings
Then smooths again for the domestic traffic of ducks.

Glasgow, July 2007

Raiders' Moon, July 2008

More than a thousand moons
Have lit this Vatersay Bay,
Ere, in a late rising
This Raiders' moon commands the eastern sky.
She softly lays, with a patina of pale gold,
A path of light leading to Beannachan.

The fusion of a hundred years
Is embraced between two rugged arms
Of land age-old beyond all telling
And brave souls long gone
Triumph with Our Lady of the Waves.

A Question

Why are we webbed with spoken words?
Must we always translate to sound
the light, the scent, the taste, the feel of things?
Let the mallard's colours be,
the bluebells in the wood,
the sweet Spring breeze that softly strokes the face.
Learn the lesson from silent swifts and swallows
that weave arcs and curves
all invisible in the May time air.

Glasgow, May 2008

To Father Hopkins

on his anniversary, 8th June

You knew the Cowcaddens:
The crowded closes in an ugly city slum:
The Irish and the Highlanders herded together
Where the Drove Road ended
And no shamrock, no heather grew.

I remember you this Sunday afternoon
In a country park you'd not have seen.
Here the Scottish gentry were housed in leisured space
Between the quiet White Cart Water
And a rising, stately avenue of trees.
In the stables no carriage horses or hunters now:
Just three Clydesdales, splendid in their patience.

A lone white iris, touched with gold,
Reminds me of you
And the purity of poetry
Forged in the furnace of your mind.

Glasgow, June 2008

November River

For Francesca and Chiara

The autumn convoy of fallen leaves
Sails midstream, in random order,
Over the reflection on dark waters
Of trees with foliage still unshed
— a glory of bronze and reddened gold.

Those colours must gild the memory
When in the long winter months
Trees stretch skeletal against the sky
And spring is but a hope yet to be revived.

Glasgow, November 2008

Walk With The Dogs

For Felicity

Grey heron fishing,
Black gull floating,
Pair of ducks swimming,
Herd of cattle cooling,
One oyster-catcher calling,
Invisible cock pheasant crowing,
Two geese drifting,
Lonely sea bird lamenting,
Distant blackbird lauding,
Smooth tide surreptitiously rising,
White butterflies fluttering,
Ancient hills sleeping,
May sun warming,
Wild flowers delicately decorating
— Mary's month in excelsis!

Seil, May 2009

At Ushaw

At measured pace the sun sets slowly,
Its yellow light gilding thin grey lines of cloud.
The woods, silent, still, are bedded in dead leaves,
While raindrops hang from each horizontal branch.
In the distance rooks fly raggedly, noisily, home to roost.
Motionless beside a gate three ponies stand.
A Mid-December day is shrinking to an early dusk.

Within doors, unseen, unheard, the Spirit stirs young hearts.

Glasgow, January 2010

Vatersay: Shortest Day 2011

The sunless solstice
fades into a deeper and deeper grey
as fine rain comes in the wind,
a wind that hurries down the hillside
to shatter the surface of the winter lochan
into little dark, dancing waves.
All is drear for the cold obsequies
Of a December day.
In all this gloom a whiteness draws the eye,
— a solitary swan.

Glasgow, January 2012

Ardmay

Arrochar, and the hill beyond
Reflected perfectly in the
Dark, still water of Loch Long.
My heart and mind are uplifted,
Alleluia, to Him, the creator God of
Yesterday, today, forever.

Glasgow, May 2014

The Old Jetty, Uidh

For Claire

An unseen sunset brings about
the gentle fading of the day,

Smooth water, mute and motionless,
lies across the Sound.

Ben Tangaval is caressed
by slow drifting cloud, thin and grey.

At intervals an oyster-catcher
shreds the silence with its piercing cry.

A lone, songless lark flies low beside the road
where slime-black slugs creep from the grass.

No moon, no stars, only the memory of the day.

Vatersay/Glasgow, July - August 2014

Pollok: The Stables Weir

For L W

Wide and still, the White Cart pauses ....
The black surface
on a windless afternoon
bears a perfect image of early autumn trees.

Lustrous and lively,
Clear water
Dances down
the Weir,
washing each stone
as it sparkles
in September sunlight.

Beyond the weir
Dark water, so briefly white,
Settles in to deep peat-brown pools
Beside the Clyde-bound current.

Glasgow, September 2014

Lunchtime Landscape

On this third November day
the Campsie Fells are patched:
patched with sunlight,
patched with shadows.
And so my life is patched:
patched with friendships,
patched with others' sorrows
until all is subsumed in Him
whose coat was without seam.

Glasgow, 3rd November 2014

Prodigal

For KD

An old man standing on the doorway
Looking down the drive.
"One day he will come back."
Short dark days of winter,
The trees stark in their leaflessness.
Spring heralded by crocus and daffodil
Before the trees burst into bud and blossom
Making Summer a sea of varied greens.
Autumn all brown and bronze and gold
With shortening days and an evening chill.
"Another year and he has not come."
Yet still an old man gazing down the drive.

Then suddenly a figure in the distance.
The figure becomes a man,
A man half-shuffling, half-limping as he comes:
His long matted hair straggling down
To shoulders part bare in very ragged rags.

The old man stumbles down the steps,
Breaks into the semblance of a run,
Arms outstretched and happiness his face.
"My son, my son, you're home!"
And total forgiveness in a tight embrace.

Gartmore, March 2015

93

Poem For A Birthday

For CC

I pause half-way up the Dun.
Above is the ethereal kingdom of the lark
which overflows with streams of song.
Below, the mass of long-stalked buttercups
is a golden field that quivers, shivers
in the could-be autumn wind.
And at the foot the West Beach tide
sweeps in with steady white-fringed waves
that stroke the long yellow width of sand.
Beyond, on the back-drop to this Hebridean scene
little shadows of little clouds
slip smoothly down the rock roughened sides of hills.

Vatersay, July 2015

Contrasts: Pollok Park

For J McC sj

Early September has a summer sun
with a hint of autumn in the wind:
luxuriant beeches are faintly turning.

Swallows swoop and swerve low over
the gently flowing peat-brown river
— flights that signal imminent farewell?

Highland cattle lie quietly chewing
whilst stabled Clydesdales tug at net bags of hay.

Water lilies sit half-closed on dark green leaves
as thistledown floats by gaily in the air.

Glasgow, September 2015

Vatersay Graveyard: 30th March, 2016

For M C

Gravestones, some upright, some at angles
Sit randomly scattered,
All names effaced into anonymity
By the Hebridean winds and rain:
No mourners now to recall them with respect or with regret.

Tread reverently to the farthest edge
Where the present has brought regimental rows,
Clear epitaphs on monumental stones.

The bright gold of solitary celandines
Punctuates the close-cropped grass
And the pale yellow of shy primroses
Softens the chill underlying thought of death
And lark-song promises yet another Spring.

Glasgow, April 2016

Seil: Late September

(Fifty words for FW's fifty years)

Two herons beside a pond:
Tall, slender, elegant
In their stillness.

Distant mountains on Mull
Stroked by the skirts of passing clouds.

A small waterfall the sole sound
In a muted landscape.

A rock as smooth to my hand
As the wind to my face.

Autumn richness in ripe blackberries.

Seil, September 2016

19th July: A Burial And A Birthday

For C C
In memoriam D D C and E Mac L

Wind-waves in the neighbouring field,
fallow and filled with self-sown charlock,
make of yellow flowers a gently moving sea.
Pale purple clover grows in solemn lines
along the oft trod path that leads
to the graveyard gate.

Vatersay's soil, sandy and soft,
affords the dead a peaceful resting place
until the Resurrection trumpet sounds.
Then will the aged arise rejuvenated,
the young their vitality and grace resume.

That our sadness may be changed to hope
we turn to the Risen Christ and Our Lady of the Waves.

(The Church on Vatersay is dedicated to Our Lady of the
Waves and St John.)

Vatersay, July – August 2017

Afterword

Eulogy for Fr Peter Banyard delivered by Dr Frank Dunn at the Requiem Mass on 20th August 2018.

It is a privilege to deliver this eulogy and I am grateful for the input of Phil Crampsey, Roddy MacLeod, Gerry McDonald, Mike McKirdy and Ronnie Renton.

Father Banyard, Father Peter, Bert, Bertie.

For me it was Fr Banyard in my early days and then Bert. Many of us have down the years received those wonderful notelets to encourage, to congratulate, to commiserate with, or to express gratitude. The ones to me were always signed "Bert SJ". I worked in New Orleans in the 1980s and from time to time attended Mass at Loyola University. Chatting to the celebrant, I mentioned that I was from Glasgow and had links with the College. I mentioned a few names of Jesuits there at the time and when I got to Father Peter Granger Banyard he replied, "Oh, Bert".

I always smiled when passing a pub in St Andrews called "Bert's Bar". I thought, "Is there no end to this man's talents?"

He was known in Vatersay as Father Peter and Mike McKirdy recalls that Bert really liked that salutation. So do I. And how appropriate, as he was a rock to so many of us.

Over 40 years ago he arrived in Barra to help out as a supply priest. He was invited to go to Vatersay which in those days was accessed only by a small ferry. The population was 100 with a tiny church and its attached one bedroom house. On his first day Bert walked the mile from the ferry slipway to the church in the rain carrying his duffle bag. When he reached the Church which looks out onto Vatersay Bay, the sun came out and he said to himself, "This will do me". He visited every house regularly and knew everyone, whether church goers or not. This was one example of, on the surface, an incongruous relationship, but one which flourished into a deep and loving bond between Father Peter and the people of Vatersay.

As Father James Crampsey said in his homily, Bert had a remarkable ability for blending into a variety of social settings. This was exemplified at Stobhill Hospital in 1994 while he was a patient in Ward 9B. An open, mixed gender, nightingale ward which included many of Springburn and Balornock's finest and which displayed the rich panoply of North Glasgow life. The patients knew everything that was going on. On weekend evenings they were offered a small libation. Lilting songs could often be heard coming from the women's end of the ward. In amongst all of this was Bert, having just suffered a heart attack. He fitted perfectly in every way and, as they say, enjoyed the banter. It was the day after my Dad died and Bert was more concerned about not going to Dad's funeral than the state of his heart. He took it in his stride when I broke the news of the need for a major heart operation. I believe his one word of reply was "GOSH"! The surgeon reckoned he would perhaps live for 10 years – but thanks to his determination, exercise and positivity Bert kicked that prediction firmly into touch. He lived an extremely active and productive further 24 years.

Bert loved his rugby and played front row into his 50s with the odd game after that. Without doubt he will have heard some words in that cauldron not found in the Ignatian Spiritual Exercises. He thrived on the spirit of the game and abhorred any questioning of the referee. On one occasion he was penalised and after the game was enjoying a pint with the ref. The ref observed that Bert had not agreed with his decision to award a penalty. "How could you possibly know that?" asked Bert. "You raised your eyebrow," came the reply.

Bert made a substantial contribution in terms of his relationship with organisations outwith Garnethill. He was a most effective forger of strong bonds with a number of rugby clubs and, in particular, West of Scotland, Hutchesons, Clarkston and the Scottish Rugby Union. He was in demand as an after dinner speaker. He also in a quiet but effective way broke down barriers with other religious organisations. This is one under-recognised aspect of Bert's many achievements.

Most important all of his achievements, of course, was his commitment to his faith and his vocation.

The list of his contributions to the school is most impressive. The Children's Fund is high on that list. Bert was the Chaplain and an integral part of that organisation for many years. He was the main contact for all the Special Needs schools and a primary school in Castlemilk with whom the Children's Fund was linked. He was a well loved guest at their Christmas parties and shows. He also made huge contributions to pastoral care, school chaplaincy, sport, alumni reunions and gardening.

And, as well writing his own poetry, Bert loved the Scottish Graffiti. One of his favourites appeared under the village sign for Crook of Devon. Somebody had written "Twinned with the thief of Baghdad".

There have been many touching tributes to Bert on Facebook. Words frequently repeated were "kind", "gentle" and "lovely man". I suspect with his love of Scottish literature he would have especially liked one which was just four words long: "Bert Banyard – Top Bloke".

Bert was a mentor, friend and go to person for family events whether happy or sad. He was much sought after for christenings, weddings and funerals. I have personal experience of his kindness following my brother John's tragic death in 2012. As the family gathered, who was there with us? Bert – gently consoling and leading us in prayer for John and us all.

Six months ago, despite his deteriorating health, Bert delivered an excellent homily in this church for Lex Wheelan with a strong and steady voice. Three months ago he wrote as fine an obituary as I have ever read for his close friend Brother Jim Spence SJ, taking the opportunity to explain to the wider world the role of a Brother and also Jim's many unsung achievements.

I mentioned previously the thoughtful notes of gratitude which many of us received from Bert. So today, Bert, the Aloysian family, your Vatersay family and so many others have the opportunity to express our gratitude to you for all you have achieved in a full and varied life characterised by service to others. May you rest in peace.